# The ARTICULATE Jazz Musician

## Mastering the Language of Jazz

Caleb Chapman & Jeff Coffin

© 2013 Alfred Music Publishing Co., Inc.
All Rights Reserved including Public Performance.
Any duplication, adaptation or arrangement of the compositions contained in this book
requires the written consent of the Publisher.
No part of this book may be photocopied or reproduced in any way without permission.
Unauthorized uses are an infringement of the U.S. Copyright Act and are punishable by law.

# ABOUT THE AUTHORS

## Caleb Chapman

As the president of Caleb Chapman Music, Caleb directs over 170 young musicians in ten elite ensembles. This includes the acclaimed Crescent Super Band, which has frequently been hailed as one of the best professional bands in the world to be comprised entirely of young musicians. In 2011 Caleb was named the "John LaPorta International Jazz Educator of the Year," one of the highest honors in music education. He has also received awards as "Best K-12 Educator" and "Best Music Educator" for the state of Utah.

Caleb's bands have been honored with 17 DownBeat Awards and featured at many of the world's most prestigious jazz festivals and venues. His program has twice received the Best of State Statue Award, marking the program as the top organization in Arts and Entertainment by surpassing every other professional music, arts, and film group in Utah for the honor. Since 2001, they have performed with over 200 guest artists, including Randy Brecker, Joe Lovano, Christian McBride, Esperanza Spalding, Peter Erskine, Toshiko Akiyoshi, Gordon Goodwin, Bob Berg, Wayne Bergeron, Dave Weckl, Nicholas Payton, Lenny Pickett, Ernie Watts, and Bob Mintzer, to name a few. Additionally, his bands have received heavy airplay on the Sirius XM "Real Jazz" Channel.

Caleb is currently a board member for the Jazz Education Network (JEN) and is a Performing Artist and Clinician for Yamaha Saxophones, Rico Reeds, and JodyJazz Mouthpieces. He currently resides in Utah with his incredible wife and four beautiful children.

www.calebchapmanmusic.com

## Jeff Coffin

Jeff Coffin is a genre-busting 3x Grammy Award-winning saxophonist, composer, bandleader, and educator. He is internationally known for his current role in the Dave Matthews Band (2008–present), as well as his 14 years as a member of Bela Fleck & the Flecktones (1997–2010). He is also very active recording and touring with his own band, Jeff Coffin & the Mu'tet. He graduated with a music education degree from the prestigious University of North Texas where he played in the acclaimed One O'Clock Lab Band.

Jeff has performed and/or recorded with a "who's who" of musicians from a wide range of styles, including Branford Marsalis, Bob Mintzer, DJ Logic, New Orleans Social Club, Maceo Parker, McCoy Tyner, Lionel Loueke, Baaba Maal, Phish, Galactic, Kirk Whalum, My Morning Jacket, Widespread Panic, Willie Nelson, Garth Brooks, Van Morrison, Vinnie Colaiuta, Tuvan throat-singers (the Alash Ensemble & Konger Ol Ondar), Del McCoury, John Scofield, Lynyrd Skynyrd, the Wailers, and many others. Jeff likes to explore the many sides of music through not only his playing but his composing as well. A number of Jeff's compositions have been published as big band arrangements and his original composition, "Zona Mona" (from the Flecktones' Outbound), was Grammy-nominated for "Best Pop Instrumental Composition" in 2001.

An engaging and passionate educator, Jeff is a heavily in-demand clinician and a Yamaha Performing Artist. Since 2001 he has presented over 300 clinics around the globe to rave reviews. In addition to his varied musical pursuits, Jeff is also a passionate photographer.

www.jeffcoffin.com

# ACKNOWLEDGMENTS

Caleb and Jeff would like to thank Victor Wooten, Roy Wooten, and Chris Walters for making the fantastic music to accompany the book. We would also like to thank Tom Giampietro (aka Tommy G), Chris Walters, Mike Seal, and Evan Wharton for preparing the rhythm charts.

Caleb thanks Alison, Porter, Bryn, Ryann, and Kate for sacrificing so much to allow me to follow my passion; my mentor and great friend Dr. Ray Smith; Rick Drumm, Robert Polan, Jim Bailey, and Rico; Jody Espina and JodyJazz Mouthpieces; Roger Eaton, John Wittmann and Yamaha Saxophones; Stephanie Kettle, Randy Morris, and the amazing young musicians of CCM past and present who have helped develop these concepts and given me the best job in the world!

Jeff thanks Alfred Publishing and all the fantastic musicians involved in this project, Yamaha Horns, John Wittmann, Jennifer Vierling, Kim Hylick, all the students and educators who will be using this book and play-a-long, my teachers past and present, and, of course, my incredible wife, Ryoko.

CD recording credits:

    Studio: House of David Recording, Nashville, TN
    Studio Engineer: Richard McLaurin
    Asst. Engineer: Jeremy Bennett
    Recorded: June 19, 2012

Photos on the front and back cover courtesy of Harry Caston.

# TABLE OF CONTENTS

All Music Composed by Jeff Coffin.
© 2001, 2012 OTANI MUSIC (BMI)
All Rights Administered by BUG MUSIC, INC., A BMG/Chrysalis Company.
This Edition (c) 2013 OTANI MUSIC (BMI)/All Rights Administered by BUG MUSIC, INC., A BMG/Chrysalis Company.
Reprinted by Permission of Hal Leonard Corporation.
All Rights Reserved.

Text by Caleb Chapman
© 2013 CHAPMAN MUSIC, INC.
All Rights Reserved. Used by Permission.

# PREFACE

As a young music educator, I struggled to find materials that would allow me to get my students off to the right start in jazz. I quickly learned that I was not alone in this frustration. While there are countless books on improvisation, there is not a single book I could locate that clearly defines jazz articulation and the basic swing concept. I was lucky enough to be able to study with the great Dr. Ray Smith at Brigham Young University who introduced me to so many of the concepts that became the foundation for my teaching. Over the years that followed, I researched and experimented until I had a method that I felt could be used successfully with even the youngest jazz students.

A while back Jeff Coffin and I were discussing the need for a book that would address articulation as the starting point for jazz instruction. In addition to being one of my absolute favorite composers and musicians, Jeff has been like a big brother to me for many years. While he spends his days playing for thousands in stadiums across the world with the Dave Matthews Band, I know that jazz education is also a top priority for him. So I can't begin to tell you how excited I was when we decided to combine his fantastic compositions and playing with my teaching experience. The resulting articulation method is designed to be used in either a private lesson or a classroom setting. The concepts are applicable and critical to all jazz musicians on any instrument.

## A Unified Approach to Articulation

Often, it seems that jazz instruction begins with improvisation concepts, rather than the foundational elements of the style. It is similar to attempting to teach a child how to build sentences in the English language or teach the rules of grammar before arming the child with a basic vocabulary.

In this book, Jeff and I have described what we believe to be an effective approach to jazz articulation and fundamentals of the style. We want to be clear that this is certainly not the only approach. Many jazz masters through the decades have approached the issue differently, which adds to the beauty of the music. However, these varied approaches also make it incredibly difficult to have tight ensemble playing without some additional instruction. For that reason, we recommend adopting this method for learning jazz. As you mature, you may decide to alter your individual approach, but this is definitely a great place to start!

*Caleb Chapman*

## A Note from Jeff

This has been a really fun journey for Caleb and me. The first time I heard Caleb's band I was truly shocked. I had never heard a high school band play like that before. I knew at that moment that Caleb had a very special and unique talent for teaching. We have been great friends ever since our first meeting. This book is an opportunity for us to explore our combined concepts of articulation while including music to play along with that is fundamentally solid with strong melodies and a rhythm section that is absolutely world-class. The band, besides myself on tenor sax, is Victor Wooten on acoustic bass, Roy "Futureman" Wooten on drum kit, and Chris Walters on piano! We think students and teachers all over the world will really dig playing along with these tracks. For each track, we have included the full quartet version as well as "music minus Jeff" version. There are also two tunes, "Tall & Lanky" and "Fruitcake," where you get to hear the band with extended solos from everyone. We are very excited that players on every continent will all have the opportunity to learn from this book and to play along with some master musicians!

The compositions are written to be fun to play, challenging, and, at the same time, educational. Don't expect to just sail right through these pages. There are some tricky passages that are specifically designed to further your technique and ability. But remember, there is nothing here you cannot play with a little work! I put a lot of thought into the compositions and we had a great time recording them for you. Caleb, Victor, Roy, Chris, and I are all very excited about the tunes and how good the grooves feel. We think you will feel the same way. I am honored to share these pages with Caleb and I hope you get as much out of this book as we all believe you will!

*Jeff Coffin*

# INTRODUCTION

In 1947, the first degree program for jazz was introduced at the college level at the University of North Texas. This may sound like a long time ago until you compare it with the hundreds of years it took for traditional music education to develop. As a result, there are still no universally accepted rules on jazz articulation, phrasing, and interpretation. While there have been some articles on the topic and mentions made in books, this is the first book dedicated in its entirety to the subject.

The language of jazz is one of the most beautiful and varied in music. Many times, because of the many complexities of jazz, young musicians and educators get so hung up on the mysteries of the music that they give up before they even get started. This book makes approaching the jazz style easy and fun. Follow the explanations, do lots of listening, practice what you have heard, and before long you too will be an ARTICULATE JAZZ MUSICIAN!

## Using the Accompanying CD

This book includes a CD with tracks for both listening and practice with Jeff Coffin and an amazing rhythm section. Each playing exercise in the book has two corresponding tracks on the accompanying CD. The first is a recording with Jeff playing the exercise on tenor saxophone as a demonstration. The second track is without the melody providing you with an opportunity to practice on your own. Although this is not meant to be an improvisation method book, you will notice that each exercise is notated with the chord changes so C, B♭, E♭ and bass clef instruments can also use the minus tracks to practice improvisation.

## The Rhythm Section

For the rhythm section books there are two important aspects: (1) Single-note lines. The piano, guitar, bass and drums books each have the music written as a single-note line for the jazz articulation examples and exercises. The piano and guitar will have a treble clef line and the bass will use the single-note line in bass clef. The drumset player will also have a single-note treble clef line. The melodic line for drumset players indicates that drummers are strongly encouraged to play the exercises on piano or a mallet instrument. To fully understand jazz articulation and what a melodic instrument player encounters, the drumset player should learn and develop the skills to play a keyboard instrument—it is vital to becoming a well-rounded drummer, percussionist, and musician!

(2) Comping. In addition to the single-note line in the rhythm section books, music for the rhythm section to comp has been provided in each rhythm section book. Comping is simply accompanying the melodic instruments—playing as a rhythm section and generally supporting the ensemble with chords, harmony, and rhythmic time. Therefore, the rhythm section players can comp as a rhythm section and/or behind horn players and soloists in a LIVE combo or big band setting. Piano and guitar comping suggestions have been provided in many units. The bass lines and drum parts are written out in all exercises.

## Getting the Most Benefit from the Book

It may be tempting to skim the "Study" section of each unit and jump to playing the exercises. But you will quickly find the mastery of the concepts will take place as you work through the "Explore" section of each unit. In these sections you will use questions, listening, improvisation, and especially practice of the jazz articulation syllables to dramatically speed the learning process.

# UNIT 1  Articulating the Jazz Language

## GOALS

In this unit, students will discover that jazz is truly a language. The jazz language is easiest to learn when approached as one would a language—step by step.

## STUDY

### Articulation in Speech

In spoken language, the clearer the articulation, the more likely it will be that people will understand you and that you will be able to understand them. Although in music we frequently refer to "articulation" exclusively as the way we start and stop notes, when referring to speech, articulation also means being able to put thoughts or feelings into words. Being an articulate jazz musician means that we can do the same thing with sound!

### Jazz is a Language

It is best to realize that jazz is a language and language allows us to communicate. As a matter of fact, because of its improvisational nature, jazz is frequently thought of as a conversation among the musicians playing together. The same techniques we would use to learn a foreign language will be the most effective in learning the language of jazz.

This book focuses on four of these techniques:

#### 1) Immerse yourself in the new language through active listening.

Would you ever expect to master a foreign language by memorizing vocabulary and some grammar rules from a textbook? Of course not! Mastering a language is a skill, not simply a list of rules and words. The same process applies to learning jazz. Jazz has always been an aural tradition, meaning it is passed from one generation to the next through listening. You will need to listen to this music to truly understand it.

#### 2) Learning the most common words first.

In his book Using your Memory, author Tony Buzan claims that just 100 words comprise 50 percent of all words used in conversation in any language. In the same way, there are a limited number of short patterns, or "licks," that make up the majority of the jazz idiom. Using the system of well-defined jazz syllables in this book, you will learn several of the most common licks that are the building blocks of jazz. These syllables replicate the tonguing principle for wind players and will be the key to mastering the style.

#### 3) Mimicking someone who has mastered the language.

The best way to learn anything is to imitate. However, all the listening in the world won't pay off unless you are able to put it into action yourself. Throughout this book, you will reference audio examples contained on the accompanying CD. While you will be using this CD in your lessons or in the classroom with your teacher, it is critical that you take time at home to practice along with the CD recording as well!

#### 4) Improvise!

Every time you open your mouth to speak, you are improvising—taking words from your vocabulary and arranging them in different ways to convey a variety of ideas, feelings, and emotions. As a child you didn't wait to speak until you had learned every word in the English language. Jazz is one of the musical languages of improvisation. So, you will learn the jazz language quicker if you begin to improvise from the beginning as well!

### One Language, Many Accents

Just as many different accents exist within a spoken language, there are many different ways to articulate jazz. For example, while Clark Terry and Clifford Brown are both legendary jazz trumpeters, their individual approach to articulation is very different. In a small ensemble setting, oftentimes you will be able to express your own style and preference for articulation. However, in a big band or jazz ensemble setting, the ensemble will never be "tight" or "clear" without a uniform approach to articulation. Without clear articulation in a big band the music comes across as "muddy"—the equivalent of mumbling in spoken language.

## EXPLORE

**1)** What is a language and how does it help us to communicate?

_____

_____

**2)** How is articulation in speech similar to articulation in music?

_____

_____

_____

_____

**3)** Let's experiment. Pick a very short poem, phrase, or sentence. Say it aloud and then play it on your instrument using the same rhythm and articulation that you would if you were speaking it. Think of the words as you are playing the notes. Choose whatever notes you want to convey meaning and emotion. Keep it simple—use only a few words and notes.

_____

_____

# UNIT 2 Say What? The Art of Active Listening

## GOALS

Students will discover that active listening is essential to being able to properly articulate the jazz language and that listening requires dedicated time and practice.

## STUDY

### Hear Ye! Hear Ye!

Active listening is just that—active! It's so much more than just having music playing in the background while you are doing other tasks. It means listening beneath, above, through, behind, around, and under the music. And, like any skill, it is one you will get better at with practice. To really learn and understand the language of jazz, listen to it every day.

### Listening Takes Time

The Greek philosopher Epictetus astutely noted, "Man has two ears but only one mouth that he might hear twice as much as he speaks." As you begin your study of jazz, that quote is a great recommendation on the amount of time you should spend actively listening. Therefore, a basic rule of thumb is to dedicate twice the amount of time to listening as you do to your playing. Be sure to schedule daily listening time just like you would for practice time on your instrument.

### Explore All Your Resources

Thanks to technology, great jazz recordings and videos are more readily available today than ever. In addition to the recordings that your school or private teacher may have available to you, many public libraries have vast collections of CDs, MP3s, and videos to loan. Additionally, there is video concert footage available online of almost every great jazz musician who has ever lived! Many online music services allow you to both sample and purchase music from the many greats of jazz.

### Open Your Ears

Similar to learning a foreign language, when you first start listening to jazz you will understand only a little or maybe even nothing at all of what you are hearing. Don't panic! Jazz is not learned in one lesson. Try not to become frustrated, and just take it step by step. As you continue to listen you will find that you can start to pick out recognizable vocabulary (licks) as well as the sound and rhythm. You will also begin to pick out the conversations between different instruments.

It is important to listen with an open mind. If you never try new foods, you may miss out on a lifetime of enjoyment. In the same way, without expanding your listening, you may never find that artist or style that eventually becomes your favorite. Also, remember that jazz is best enjoyed live. While recordings are fantastic, there's nothing like experiencing the music with the musicians in the moment and space they are creating it.

## EXPLORE

CD TRACK 1 Let's get started listening to jazz. Check out the quartet playing Jeff's composition, "Tall & Lanky."

**1)** With your class or your teacher, discuss any emotions or mood the piece conveys to you. Does it make you think of any particular color, object, or visual scene (like a movie)?

_____

**2)** Listen to some of the same track again and this time, focus on only one instrument for the whole time. Does it evoke any different emotions or ideas from the first listen?

_____

**3)** Now that you have heard it twice, can you identify all the instruments in the recording?

_____

**4)** Come up with five words that describe the track or that you would associate with it (for example: fast, interesting, fun, loud, clear, peaceful, and so on).

_____

**5)** Why is active listening important to learning jazz?

_____

**6)** How is listening to music with others a helpful exercise?

_____

**7)** What are the listening resources you have access to?

_____

## UNIT 3 It Don't Mean a Thing—Basic Swing Conception

### GOALS

This unit is focused on beginning to discover, learn, and understand the rhythmic concept of swing eighth notes. In addition, to discover and understand the legato nature of eighth note lines in jazz.

### STUDY

#### Swing it!

Swinging simply refers to the concept of playing the downbeat (or on-beat) eighth notes longer than the offbeat eighth notes, which gives the music a "lilting" sound. Traditionally in jazz, even though the eighth notes should be played unevenly, they are notated (written) as equal eighth notes.

The length of the notes in relation to each other varies at different tempos. At slower speeds, the notes are more uneven. At higher speeds or tempos, the notes become more similar in length. At a medium tempo, it is best to think of two eighth notes being played as an eighth note triplet where the first two notes are tied together.

*Key Concept*

**In swing music, the downbeat eighth note is always longer in duration than the offbeat eighth note. This is the case even if a phrase starts on the offbeat.**

*Key Concept*

**Space in an eighth note line is the enemy of swing!**

## It's All "Smooth" Jazz

Many young musicians think of jazz as heavily accented music with lots of attack. It is just the opposite. Jazz is mostly a very legato (connected) musical style. Any space in the eighth note lines of a swing arrangement or "chart" will negatively impact the proper style of the music. It is this space that creates a very corny-sounding "ricky-ticky" effect or sound frequently heard in inexperienced ensembles.

Often in concert band instruction for wind instruments, we talk about a TA syllable to help understand articulation. In jazz, we will have more success using the DA (pronounced "DAH") syllable.

## EXPLORE

**1)** What is the difference in tongue placement between the syllables TA and DA?

_____

**2)** Why does this use of the DA syllable make a difference in the sound that is produced?

_____

## PLAY

In this short music example, be sure to swing the eighth notes and play the articulations exactly as written. Remember, even though you will use a DA tongue in the phrases, there should be no space between notes.

Eb Instrument

# UNIT 4   The Jazz Articulation Rule—DA and AH syllables

## GOALS

Students discover and work to memorize the Jazz Articulation Rule so they have a clear understanding of this important aspect of jazz articulation. Students can review and practice with the most common jazz syllables, DA and AH, and understand the difference between these two syllables.

## STUDY

### The Rule

When it comes to jazz articulation, it all boils down to one simple rule:

> **_Always slur from the offbeat eighth note to the downbeat eighth note._**

That's it—one rule. If you can remember this, you are already well on your way to becoming an articulate jazz musician!

*Key Concept*

**The Jazz Articulation Rule applies ONLY to eighth notes. With rare exception, longer notes will all be articulated. Note: there are a few other exceptions to the rule we'll discuss later.**

### The First Two Jazz Syllables

As mentioned in Unit 1, you will be using syllables to master the jazz language. The first is the syllable for an articulated note: DA. Notice how when you say "DA" the sound begins with the tongue and the "D" sound. The next syllable to learn is for slurred notes: the AH syllable. It's easy!

In the following exercise there are no articulation markings. So, how do you know what to articulate? Start by applying the jazz articulation rule to the eighth notes by articulating the offbeat eighth notes and slur to the downbeat eighth notes.

What is a phrase? A phrase is a grouping of consecutive melodic notes. Another explanation is any group of notes with silence on either end. An analogy to language text would be a sentence. Each phrase in this exercise starts with an articulated (DA) note. Also, in this exercise, any notes longer than an eighth note should all be articulated by using the DA syllable.

## EXPLORE

Compose (yes, write the notes!) eight measures of rhythm—use only eighth notes, half notes, and whole notes. Do not use any rests. And be able to say the jazz syllables for the rhythm you notate. Keep it simple by using only three or four pitches. You can write on the same line or space or vary the notes, your choice.

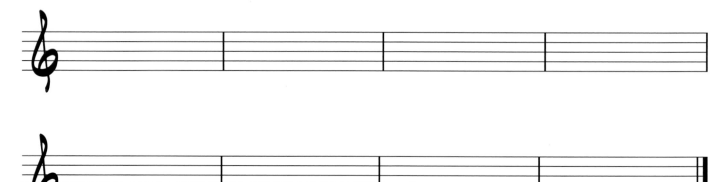

In the space provided below the notes, write in the proper jazz syllables for the exercise in this unit. When you have it correct, say the syllables for the entire exercise in a medium tempo with a metronome or someone keeping the beat.

## PLAY

Play the Unit 4 Exercise, "Strollin'."

**CD Use:** For the Unit Exercises (Units 4–17) on the CD, each unit includes two tracks for each unit. A DEMO track with tenor sax, piano, bass, and drums. This track is provided so all students can listen, learn, and imitate the articulation, phrasing, and style of the professional musicians. The PLAY-ALONG track is minus the melody saxophone so that student can play along with the professional rhythm section.

# Strollin'

# UNIT 5   Jazz Articulation Rule Exception #1—DU and DOT syllables

## GOALS

Students discover and recognize the DU and DOT jazz syllables. They should also work to describe and understand why these two syllables are an exception to the Jazz Articulation Rule.

## STUDY

### Two New Syllables

While there is only one rule you need to remember for jazz articulation, there are a few exceptions. To understand the first exception, let's learn two new syllables, DOT and DU.

In jazz, DOT (pronounced "DAHT") is used for an accented note that has an articulated start and end. For wind players, this means the note both starts and ends with the tongue. For rhythm section players, it means playing the note detached but with full value—not staccato or too short.

### DOT is used in two instances:

**1)** For all quarter notes (unless notated otherwise)

**2)** For any eighth note followed by a rest

Although accented, DOT is not a short note—it should receive full rhythmic value.

DU (pronounced "DOO") is used for an eighth note that is articulated but has a softer volume than the notes around it. Any eighth note immediately preceding a DOT will be DU.

These two new syllables are the first exception to the Jazz Articulation Rule as they will always be articulated, whether or not they occur on the downbeat or offbeat. Take a look at the Unit 5 Example. This example clearly illustrates the DU and DOT syllables in action with eighth notes.

It's easy, just **sing** this example:

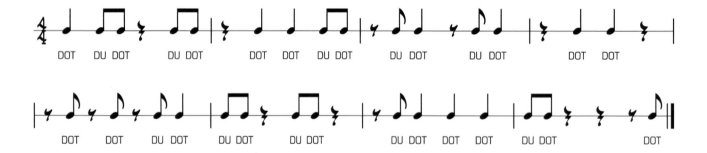

## EXPLORE

**1)** Compose eight measures of rhythm utilizing only eighth notes, quarter notes, and rests. Be able to say the jazz syllables for the rhythm you notate. You can use only one line or space or vary it, your choice.

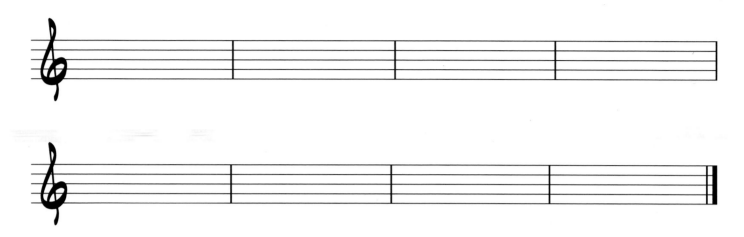

**2)** In the space provided below the notes in the Unit 5 Exercise, write in the proper jazz syllables for this unit. When you have it correct, say the syllables for the entire exercise in time (tempo) with a metronome or someone keeping the beat.

## PLAY

Play the Unit 5 Exercise, "One More Once."

# One More Once

This page left blank to facilitate page turns.

# UNIT 6 Articulating the Release

## GOALS

In this unit, students discover that cut-offs or releases are equally important to note attacks. Students will also work to be able to properly interpret note lengths from written music.

## STUDY

### Finish What You Start

You have learned quite a bit about starting notes. Now it's time to focus on cutoffs or the release of your notes. This concept virtually doubles the power and impact of a band by adding the same definition to the releases as the attacks.

In concert band settings, cutting off notes with the tongue by the wind players is highly discouraged. However, in jazz a tongue cut-off by the saxophones and brass is frequently required. As you say the syllable DOT, you will notice that you must use the tongue to complete the syllable.

For reed players, a tongue cut-off involves touching the tip of the tongue to the tip of the reed. For brass players, the tongue should be touched to the inside of the front teeth. Rhythm section players can attain a similar sound by muting their strings or cymbals. Also, while you will use DA for most long notes, and this syllable does not have a tongue cut-off, wind players may use a light tongue cut-off at the end of the note to give added definition.

### Interpreting Length

It is critical that each member of an ensemble give the same length to the notated music. As a general rule, long notes followed by a rest should be cut off on the following beat.

Sometimes a composer or publisher will add an eighth note tied to the long note to indicate this.

## EXPLORE

**1)** Why is it important to focus on the release of notes in addition to the start of the note?

_____

_____

**2)** In the spaces provided below the notes, write in the proper jazz syllables for the Unit 6 Exercise. When you have it correct, say the syllables for the entire exercise in time with a metronome or someone keeping the beat.

## PLAY

Play the Unit 6 Exercise, "The Big Giant."

*Key Concept*

**As lower instruments (trombones, baritone sax, etc.) tend to "ring" longer, they will need to play slightly shorter for a uniform cut off with the ensemble.**

# The Big Giant

DOT DOT DOT   DOT DA   DU DOT DOT DOT   DA DA AH DA DA

DOT DOT DOT   DOT DA   DU DOT DOT DOT   DA DA AH DA DA

# UNIT 7  Review DA, AH, DU and DOT Syllables

## GOALS

In this unit, review all the syllables learned so far—DA, AH, DU, and DOT. Play and sing the Unit 7 Exercise. Remember to be precise on cutoffs and articulating the release of the notes.

## PLAY

Play the Unit 7 Exercise, "Just Say NOLA."

Just Say NOLA

TRACK 8 Demo
TRACK 9 Play-Along Track

# UNIT 8  Jazz Articulation Rule Exception #2—Accenting Tops of Contour

## GOALS

Students discover how to recognize a downbeat top of contour note, and will learn how to articulate it and understand why it is an exception to the Jazz Articulation Rule.

## STUDY

### Jazz in 3-D

Music without contrast is boring, and jazz is no exception. You can add contrast and excitement by emphasizing (accenting) notes. You have already learned to accent notes at the end of phrases (DOT). Because of the Jazz Articulation Rule (slurring from offbeat to downbeat), it is tempting to simply accent every other note. However, in the jazz language, the top notes of the contour receive the accent. This effect moves jazz from a two-dimensional or flat sound to a three-dimensional, much more exciting sound!

In any eighth note phrase, there can be several contours. The top note of the contour is identified simply by seeing if the notes on either side are lower.

Although we normally slur to downbeat eighth notes, when the top note of the contour is an eighth note on the downbeat we accent and articulate it. This may be the most difficult concept in jazz articulation because if you are reading a chart it requires you to visually scan ahead while you are playing.

*Key Concept*

**The top of contour exception only applies to notes that occur in the middle of an eighth note line and fall on a downbeat.**

## EXPLORE

**1)** Why do we articulate the top note of a contour when it occurs on the downbeat?

_____

_____

**2)** Why does the top of contour exception only apply to downbeat eighth notes in the middle of the phrase?

_____

_____

**3)** In the space provided, write in the proper jazz syllables for the Unit 8 Exercise. When you have it correct, say the syllables for the entire exercise in time with a metronome or someone keeping the beat.

## PLAY

Play the Unit 8 Exercise, "Dexter's Hat."

# Dexter's Hat

# UNIT 9  Jazz Articulation Rule Exception #3—DU-WAH Syllables

## GOALS

Students discover how to recognize and properly articulate the DU-WAH combination of jazz syllables. This includes muting the DU note and accenting the WAH note.

## STUDY

### Do What?

It is time to learn the fifth syllable used in jazz articulation, WAH. For our purposes, WAH will always be preceded by DU. DU-WAHs are fairly easy to spot. They occur when an eighth note on a downbeat is followed by a long note on the offbeat.

> **Key Concept**
>
> Although WAH is accented, it is not articulated.

Check out this musical example:

You will remember that DU represents a softer note. WAH differs from the other non-articulated syllable, AH, in that it is accented. How do you accent without using the tongue? By using more volume. This will be easier for a wind instrument than a rhythm instrument but the concept is the same. Just like the combination of DU-DOT covered previously, DU-WAH adds exciting contrast to a piece by moving from a softer note to a louder one.

The WAH is always slurred, and, since the WAH always occurs on an offbeat, this makes the DU-WAH an exception to the Jazz Articulation Rule.

### Here's the Scoop

When a DU-WAH is notated on the same pitch, the effect is achieved for wind players by "scooping" into the second note. For saxophonists, this is typically done with the jaw. For trumpet players, the scoop can be done with the half-valve technique or lip bend. Trombone players can use the slide for this effect. Guitarists and bass players will simply "bend" the string.

> **Key Concept**
>
> Although it may be tempting, do not scoop on DU-WAHs when they are not the same pitch.

## EXPLORE

**1)** How is it possible to accent a note without articulating it?

_____

_____

**2)** In the space provided, write in the proper jazz syllables for the Unit 9 Exercise. When you have it correct, say the syllables for the entire exercise in time with a metronome or someone keeping the beat.

## PLAY

Play the Unit 9 Exercise, "Jump on the Bus."

# Jump on the Bus

# UNIT 10  Review DA, AH, DU, DOT, and WAH syllables

## GOALS

Let's review all the syllables we have learned so far—DA, AH, DU, DOT, and the final basic syllable, WAH. Without writing any syllables in, play and sing the Unit 10 Exercise. Work to identify all eighth note tops of contour and accent them. Don't forget to accent the WAH syllable.

## PLAY

Play the Unit 10 Exercise, "Coco's Blues."

Coco's Blues

TRACK 14 Demo
TRACK 15 Play-Along Track

# UNIT 11  3 Is a Magic Number—Articulating Triplets

## GOALS

Students discover the articulation and proper jazz syllables for eighth note triplets and quarter-note triplets.

## STUDY

### Eighth Note Triplets

Jazz musicians through the years have found multiple ways to successfully articulate eighth note triplets. Legendary jazz trumpeter Clifford Brown, for example, would frequently articulate the first and second note of each set. While there seems to exist no exact right or wrong way to approach eighth note triplets in jazz, for the sake of a unified approach we recommend you articulate the first of each set of eighth note triplets found in the middle of a phrase. The syllables for this are DA-AH-LA (LAH), as shown below.

Check out Example #1

A set of eighth note triplets before a rest (at the end of the phrase) are all articulated like regular eighth notes before a rest. So you will use the syllables DA-DU-DOT when singing the figure.

Check out Example #2

### Quarter Note Triplets

Unless marked otherwise, quarter note triplets in jazz should always be played full length, articulated, and accented. You will use the DA syllable for most quarter note triplets, although a quarter note triplet figure followed by a rest will have a DOT at the end.

Check out Example #3

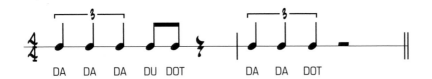

> **Key Concept**
>
> **Although quarter note triplets are accented, they do not end with a tongue cut-off unless they are followed by a rest.**

## EXPLORE

**1)** When playing triplet figures in jazz, is the tendency to drag or to rush?

_____

**2)** In the space provided, write in the proper jazz syllables for the Unit 11 exercise. When you have it correct, say the syllables for the entire exercise in time with a metronome or someone keeping the beat.

## PLAY

Play the Unit 11 Exercise, "Triple Agents."

# Triple Agents

SWING ♩ = 90

DA DA AH LA DA DOT    DA DA AH LA DA DOT    DA DA AH LA DOT DU WAH_____

DA DA DA DA DA DA ____

Double Your Pleasure—Articulating in a Double-Time Feel

## GOALS

Students discover will how to apply previously learned articulation concepts to double-time feel passages.

## STUDY

### Keep It Moving

Often in medium or slow tempo pieces, a composer or soloist (while improvising) will double the speed of the piece to add excitement. While the melody and time in the rhythm section are sped up, the chord progression or underlying harmony continues at the exact same speed as previously. This is referred to as a double-time feel.

To articulate in a double-time feel, you will need to apply all the rules you have already learned, but apply them to the halved-values. In other words, the rules that apply normally to eighth notes would be applied to sixteenths, and the rules that apply normally quarter notes would now be applied to eighth notes.

## EXPLORE

**1)** What is the difference between double-time and a double-time feel?

_____

_____

**2)** In the space provided, write in the proper jazz syllables for the Unit 12 Exercise. When you have it correct, say the syllables for the entire exercise in time with a metronome or someone keeping the beat.

## PLAY

Play the Unit 12 Exercise, "Twice as Nice."

This page left blank to facilitate page turns.

# Twice as Nice

DOT DA DA AH DA AH DA AH DA AH DA DA DU DOT      DA DU DOT

DOT DA DA AH DA DA DA AH DA AH DA DA DU WAH_____ DOT

DA DA DU DOT

DA DU DOT

DA DA AH DU DOT

30

# UNIT 13  Jazz Articulation Rule Exception #4—Ghosted Notes

## GOALS

In this unit, students discover ghosted notes, recognize and understand the notation for a ghosted note, and play it accurately. They should also be able to identify notes that should be ghosted that may not be marked in the music.

## STUDY

### Using Less Volume to Accent

Like a DU preceding a WAH or DOT, ghosted (or swallowed) notes are used to emphasize the notes around them by dropping in volume, but the drop is much more exaggerated than a DU. In fact, they are normally played with hardly any sound at all and verge on being inaudible.

To ghost a note, wind players simply reduce the amount of air they are putting through the horn. Bass and guitar players can mute the string for a similar effect. In an ensemble, saxophones typically do not need to ghost as much as brass and can help fill in the sound if brass players are getting too quiet for technical reasons. The jazz syllable you will use for a ghosted note is NN.

Check out Example #1

### Spot the Ghost

If a composer wants you to ghost a note, it will be indicated with an "x" in place of the note head or by placing parenthesis around the note. In addition to those that are notated, you will frequently find other notes that sound like they should be ghosted. Follow your instinct on these. Many times, the bottom note of the contour of a line will be ghosted.

Also, in an eighth note phrase, any note between two downbeat tops of contour will always be ghosted.

Check out Example #2

*Key Concept*

**Ghosted notes should always be slurred, and they almost always occur on an offbeat. This makes ghosted notes an exception to the Jazz Articulation Rule.**

## EXPLORE

**1)** How do ghosted notes add excitement and energy to the music?

_____

_____

**2)** In the space provided, write in the proper jazz syllables for the Unit 14 Exercise. When you have it correct, say the syllables for the entire exercise in time with a metronome or someone keeping the beat.

## PLAY

Play the Unit 13 Exercise, "Fats Wailer."

# Fats Wailer

## UNIT 14   Review Triplets, Double-Time Feel, and Ghosted Notes

### GOALS

Review the skills learned in the last three units—triplets, double-time feel, and ghosted notes. Carefully observe the Unit 14 Exercise and look for and identify (1) the triplets—both quarter note and eighth note triplets; (2) examples of double-time feel sections; and (3) ghosted notes that may not be identified with an "x."

### PLAY

Play the Unit 14 Exercise, "Slinky Sideways."

Slinky Sideways

TRACK 22  Demo
TRACK 23  Play-Along Track

35

# UNIT 15  Funk and Rock

## GOALS

Students discover that funk and rock styles employ straight eighth notes on the melody or "head." Students should understand that there are two generally accepted ways to articulate this style and understand them both.

## STUDY

### Play That Funky Music

In contrast to everything you have worked on to this point, the melodies or "heads" in funk and rock are played straight (without swinging the eighth notes). In other words, written eighth notes are played evenly. This is the main difference compared to the swing charts you have been working on. In fact, DU-WAHs and DU-DOTs can and should be applied in exactly the same way—although they will not be swung. This means the DU syllables will be softer and the WAHs and DOTs will be accented.

Funk articulation can generally be approached in one of two ways. One option is to articulate every eighth note. The other, which is what you will hear on the play-along CD, is to apply the Jazz Articulation Rule and slur from offbeat eighth notes to downbeat eighth notes in the phrase. While either way is appropriate, however, it is critical that all musicians agree on the same approach when playing together.

*Key Concept*

**There are multiple ways to approach funk and rock articulation. Be sure all musicians have agreed on one of them!**

## EXPLORE

**1)** What is the main difference between the funk style and the swing style?

_____

_____

**2)** What are the two main articulation approaches for the funk style?

_____

_____

## PLAY

Play the Unit 15 Exercise, "A Little Something."

# A Little Something

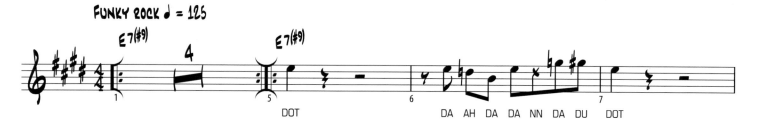

# UNIT 16   Other Articulation Effects and Embellishments

## GOALS

Students discover and recognize, notate, and properly play DOITs, falls, glissandos, and shakes.

## STUDY

### More Tools for the 'Shed

In addition to the standard jazz articulations you have already learned, there are several common effects and embellishments that you will also come across. While you find descriptions of each of these below, there is no way to fully understand the proper way to play them without listening. And, there is no way to master them without "hitting the woodshed" and practicing.

## DOIT

The DOIT (pronounced "doyt") is accomplished for wind instruments by articulating the notated pitch and then forcing the pitch up as much as an octave (or sometimes more). Saxophones will do this by quickly moving chromatically up by fingering pitches combined with a changing shape in the oral cavity. Trumpets accomplish this with a combination of "lipping," "flying fingers," and half-valves. Trombones will use the lip and slide. The duration of the DOIT is determined by the length and shape of the marking in the music. No individual pitches should be heard after the initial attack.

### Fall

The fall (or drop) is basically the opposite of the DOIT. The musician should articulate the pitch and then force the pitch down as much as an octave. The duration and speed vary depending on the piece and can often be determined by the marking. The technique for each instrument to accomplish this is similar to that listed above. In a large ensemble setting, no instrument should fall longer than the lead player in the section or the lead trumpet. While falls may be played diatonically (in the scale) or chromatically, frequently no individual pitches should be heard after the initial attack.

### Glissando

The glissando, or "gliss," is typically a fast chromatic run between two notated pitches. It is usually out of time and should be played in a legato manner, only articulating the first note. Again, no individual notes should be heard in a gliss after the initial attack. It is important to understand that while the placement of the written note still occurs as notated, the gliss is an ornament and does not take away any duration of the written note. If a gliss is written leading up to a quarter note on beat 1, then the written quarter note is played or attacked right on beat 1—the gliss occurs prior to the note.

### Shake

The shake is a rapid trill between two pitches. For saxophone and rhythm section players, the trill is between the written pitch and a minor third above it (unless otherwise notated). For brass players, the shake is a lip trill between the written pitch and the next highest overtone.

You will see each of these effects in the Unit 16 Exercise.

## EXPLORE

**1)** What purpose do effects in a jazz chart serve?

_____

_____

**2)** What are some other effects you have heard used in recordings?

_____

_____

## PLAY

Play the Unit 16 Exercise, "What's Up, What's Down?"

# What's Up, What's Down?

TRACK 26 Demo
TRACK 27 Play-Along Track

## UNIT 17 Overall Review

### GOALS

This exercise serves as an overview or master review. It covers all the concepts introduced in this book and provides students a chance to show that they have a clear understanding of basic jazz articulation. The good news is there are no surprises or tricks in the Unit 17 Exercise. Every note should be recognizable and identifiable based on the rules and exercises you have studied, played, and hopefully learned. Don't worry about writing in any jazz syllables, but do try to remember all the articulation you have learned. But the most important thing is to just have fun and play some jazz!

### PLAY

Play the Unit 17 Exercise, "Wrappin' Up."

## Wrappin' Up

TRACK 28 Demo
TRACK 29 Play-Along Track

As a bonus, check out CD Track 30—it's Jeff Coffin and the quartet playing Jeff's composition, "Fruitcake."

## APPENDIX A   Glossary

**AH**—Jazz articulation syllable used for a slurred eighth note.

**Big band**—A large jazz ensemble with one player per part that typically includes saxes, trumpets, trombones, and a rhythm section of piano, guitar, bass, and drums.

**Bar**—In music, another name for a measure.

**Blues**—A type of form; usually comprised of three phrases over twelve bars.

**Changes**—The chord progression of a composition; sometimes referred to as harmonic motion.

**Chart**—In jazz, the written composition or arrangement (sheet music).

**Chops**—Slang for a high level of musical ability and technical facility.

**Chorus**—A full cycle through the form of a jazz composition.

**Combo**—A small jazz ensemble usually comprised of a rhythm section with one or more horns and/or a vocalist.

**Comping**—Short for "accompanying"; refers to the rhythmic and harmonic patterns typically played by the chordal instruments in a rhythm section, including piano, guitar, and vibes.

**DA (DAH)**—The most common jazz articulation syllable that begins with an attack but does not end with one.

**DIT**—A jazz articulation syllable that is accented and starts and ends with an attack; represents a "short" note and typically does not receive full value.

**DOIT**—A jazz articulation effect accomplished for wind instruments by articulating the notated pitch and then forcing the pitch up as much as an octave or more.

**DOT (DAHT)**—A jazz articulation syllable that is accented and starts and ends with an attack; receives full value.

**Double-time feel**—A technique in which performers play twice as fast as the original tempo of a tune but maintain the length of the harmonic progression.

**Downbeat**—The longer, first part of a beat; if you are tapping your foot, it is when your foot goes down.

**DU (DOO)**—A jazz articulation syllable that is softer than the notes around it; starts with an attack and precedes DOT and WAH.

**DU-WAH (DOO-WAH)**—Jazz articulation syllables that occur when there is an eighth note on a down beat followed by a long note on the off beat; the second note is both slurred and accented.

**Fall**—A jazz articulation effect accomplished by articulating the pitch and then forcing the pitch down as much as an octave.

**Funk**—A style of music with a strong rhythmic groove.

**Ghosted note**—Note that is much softer than the notes around it; often felt more than heard; has a specific rhythmic value but little or no distinguishable pitch.

**Glissando (or Gliss)**—An articulation effect that is typically a fast chromatic run between two notated pitches.

**Head**—The main melody of a song.

**Improvisation (or Improv)**—In jazz, spontaneously creating new melodies.

**Lick**—A short musical phrase or idea.

**Melody**—The main theme of a piece of music.

**Muddy**—Expression used to describe a band that is not playing together or articulating in a uniform manner.

**Offbeat**—The shorter, second part of a beat; if you are tapping your foot, it is after your foot goes up.

**Phrase**—Any group of notes with silence on either end, or a grouping of consecutive melodic notes.

**Release**—To stop or end the note, a cut-off.

**Rhythm section**—Typically guitar, bass, piano, drums, and occasionally, vibes.

**Riff**—A short, melodic phrase.

**Shake**—An articulation effect accomplished by a rapid trill between two pitches.

**Solo**—A section where one instrument is featured and the material they play is usually improvised.

**Straight-eighths**—Even (not swung) eighth notes.

**Swallowed note**—Another name for a ghosted note (see above).

**Swing eighth notes**—Uneven eighth notes where the downbeat eighth note is longer and the offbeat eighth note is shorter; creates a lilting effect.

**Swing style**—A style of jazz characterized by uneven eighth notes where the downbeats are held longer than the offbeats.

**Tight**—When a band is playing precise rhythms as a group.

**Transcribe**—The process of notating a melody or improvised solo.

**Top of contour**—Refers to an eight note which is surrounded by lower notes on either side; should be accented.

**Woodshed**—To practice a musical concept until mastered.

## APPENDIX B   Basic Jazz Articulation Syllable Quick-Guide

### Jazz Articulation Rule

Always slur from the offbeat eigth note to the downbeat eighth note

### Jazz Articulation Rule Exceptions

**1)** Always tongue DU and DOT

**2)** Always tongue (and accent) tops of contour

**3)** Always slur DU-WAH

**4)** Always slur ghosted notes

### Basic Jazz Syllables

Two Types:

**1)** Tongued—DA, DOT, DU

**2)** Slurred—AH, WAH

### Jazz Syllable Identification

How do you know what syllable to use for each note? Select a note in your music and proceed through the following questions beginning with #1 in the Basic Jazz Syllables indicated above. If the answer is YES, use the syllable(s) to the right. If the answer is NO, proceed to the next question. You should be able to assign every note in your music one of these syllables. After you have mastered them verbally, you'll need to think the syllables as you play to get the proper articulation.

**1)** Is it ♪ followed by a long note starting on the downbeat?  DU-WAH

**2)** Is it ♪, the last eighth note of a triplet, or the last quarter note of a triplet immediately followed by a rest? Is it a quarter note?  DOT

**3)** Is it ♪ immediately followed by DOT?  DU

**4)** Is it a slurred ♪ (see Articulation Rule above)?  AH

**5)** Anything else (including notes longer than a quarter note)?  DA

# Jazz Play-Alongs

Go beyond the typical play-along with Alfred's Jazz Play-Along series, an innovative approach to teaching improvisation! Each tune has specific improvisation tips and suggestions with a sample solo that makes learning how to improv easier. The play-along tracks allow a soloist or group to learn and perform with the rhythm section only. Play-alongs have never been more complete!

- **Parts for C, B-Flat, E-Flat, and bass clef instruments**
- **Separate book for rhythm section instruments**
- **Written-out and recorded solo examples**
- **Plenty of choruses for soloing opportunities**
- **Specific tips and suggestions for each tune**
- **CD with demo and play-along tracks recorded by top musicians**

## Alfred's Jazz Play Along Series

### Vol. 1: Strayhorn & More

**Titles:** *Take the 'A' Train • Isfahan • Freddy Freeloader • Caravan • Prelude to a Kiss • Johnny Come Lately • UMMG (Upper Manhattan Medical Group) • Raincheck • Chelsea Bridge.*

(00-33387) C, B-Flat, E-Flat & Bass Clef Instruments Book & CD
(00-38722) Rhythm Section (Piano, Bass, Drum Set) Book & MP3 CD

### Vol. 2: Swingin' Now

**Titles:** *Stella by Starlight • On Green Dolphin Street • Have You Met Miss Jones? • Bye Bye Blackbird • What Is This Thing Called Love? • Days of Wine and Roses • I Got Rhythm • Stompin' at the Savoy • Just Friends.*

(00-33390) C, B-Flat, E-Flat & Bass Clef Instruments Book & CD
(00-38725) Rhythm Section (Piano, Bass, Drum Set) Book & MP3 CD

### Vol. 3: Brubeck & More

**Titles:** *Alone Together • Good Bait • How High the Moon • In Your Own Sweet Way • Invitation • It's a Raggy Waltz • Old Devil Moon • Robbin's Nest • Unit 7.*

(00-36093) C, B-Flat, E-Flat & Bass Clef Instruments Book & CD
(00-36096) Rhythm Section (Piano, Bass, Drum Set) Book & MP3 CD

### Vol. 4: The Music of Gordon Goodwin

**Titles:** *Count Bubba's Revenge • High Maintenance • Howdiz Songo? • Jazz Police • Maynard & Waynard • Race to the Bridge • Rippin 'n Runnin' • That's How We Roll • The Very Best of Times.*

(00-36099) C, B-Flat, E-Flat & Bass Clef Instruments Book & CD
(00-36102) Rhythm Section (Piano, Bass, Drum Set) Book & MP3 CD

## Alfred's Jazz Easy Play Along Series

### Vol. 1: Easy Standards

**Titles:** *Ain't Misbehavin' • Blue Train • Impressions • Killer Joe • Jive Samba • Little Sunflower • My Little Suede Shoes • Perdido • Work Song.*

(00-36081) C, B-Flat, E-Flat & Bass Clef Instruments Book & CD
(00-36084) Rhythm Section (Piano, Bass, Drum Set) Book & MP3 CD

### Vol. 2: Easy Standards

**Titles:** *After You've Gone • Blues March • Lazy Bird • Lester Leaps In • Mr. PC • Road Song • Scrapple From the Apple • St. James Infirmary • Summertime.*

(00-36087) C, B-Flat, E-Flat & Bass Clef Instruments Book & CD
(00-36090) Rhythm Section (Piano, Bass, Drum Set) Book & MP3 CD

### Vol. 3: Easy Latin Standards

**Titles:** *Gentle Rain • Listen Here • Manha de Carnival • Night and Day • Poinciana • Recorda Me • The Shadow of Your Smile • Softly, as in a Morning Sunrise • Star Eyes.*

(00-38953) C, B-Flat, E-Flat & Bass Clef Instruments Book & CD
(00-38956) Rhythm Section (Piano, Bass, Drum Set) Book & MP3 CD

**alfred.com**